Animals vs. Humans

RODENTS INFEST

Elisabeth Herschbach

WWW.APEXEDITIONS.COM

Apex is distributed by North Star Editions:
sales@northstareditions.com | 888-417-0195

Produced for Apex by Red Line Editorial.

Photographs ©: iStockphoto, cover, 1, 4–5, 10–11, 16–17, 28–29, 52–53; Shutterstock Images, 6–7, 8–9, 12–13, 14–15, 18–19, 20–21, 22–23, 24–25, 26–27, 30–31, 32–33, 40–41, 42–43, 44–45, 49, 50–51, 54–55, 56–57; David Gray/Getty Images News/Getty Images, 34–35; Rick Rycroft/AP Images, 37; Rouelle Umali/Imago/Alamy, 38–39; Pius Utomi Ekpei/AFP/Getty Images, 46–47; Red Line Editorial, 58–59

Library of Congress Control Number: 2023922208

ISBN
979-8-89250-212-2 (hardcover)
979-8-89250-233-7 (paperback)
979-8-89250-274-0 (ebook pdf)
979-8-89250-254-2 (hosted ebook)

Printed in the United States of America
Mankato, MN
082024

NOTE TO PARENTS AND EDUCATORS

Apex books are designed to build literacy skills in striving readers. Exciting, high-interest content attracts and holds readers' attention. The text is carefully leveled to allow students to achieve success quickly.

TABLE OF CONTENTS

Chapter 1

MICE INVADE

A family can't sleep at night. Mice are everywhere in their apartment. The rodents dart across the floor. They make nests in cabinets. They leave smelly droppings and urine everywhere. Their scratching keeps the family awake.

Mice crawling or digging inside walls can sound like scratching.

Mice can enter homes through gaps around windows, pipes, and wires.

Soon, the family's son has trouble breathing. His mother takes him to the hospital. The doctor says his asthma is being made worse by the mice. The doctor tells the mother to call the health department. They can send an exterminator to control the mice.

'TIS THE SEASON

Mice infestations are worst when it's cold. In the winter, mice look for a warm place to shelter. They squeeze in through cracks and holes in buildings. They can fit into spaces that are as small as a dime.

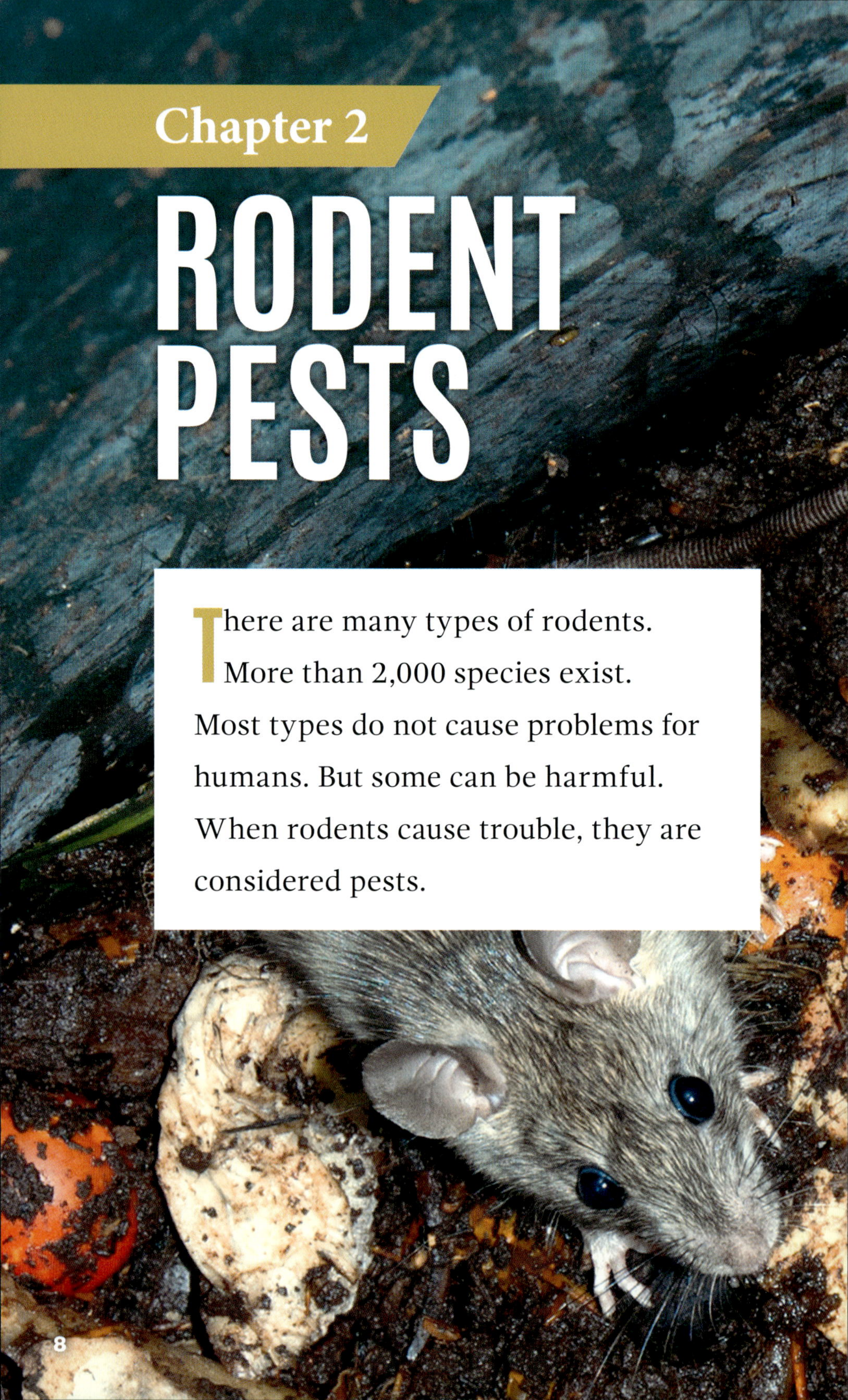

Chapter 2

RODENT PESTS

There are many types of rodents. More than 2,000 species exist. Most types do not cause problems for humans. But some can be harmful. When rodents cause trouble, they are considered pests.

Many farms lose food to rodents. But only about 10 percent of rodent species are farm pests.

Mice and rats are the most common rodent pests. They enter human spaces to find food and shelter. Mice and rats are a big problem in crowded cities. More people leads to more trash. That means there's more food for rodents.

SIGHTSEEING RATS

Every year, many tourists visit the Colosseum. This ancient site is in Rome, Italy. In 2023, the Colosseum also had some unwelcome visitors. Rats came. They found the trash left behind by tourists. It led to an infestation.

Rodents in cities eat almost anything. They even eat rotting meat.

Two mice can lead to hundreds of mice after just eight months.

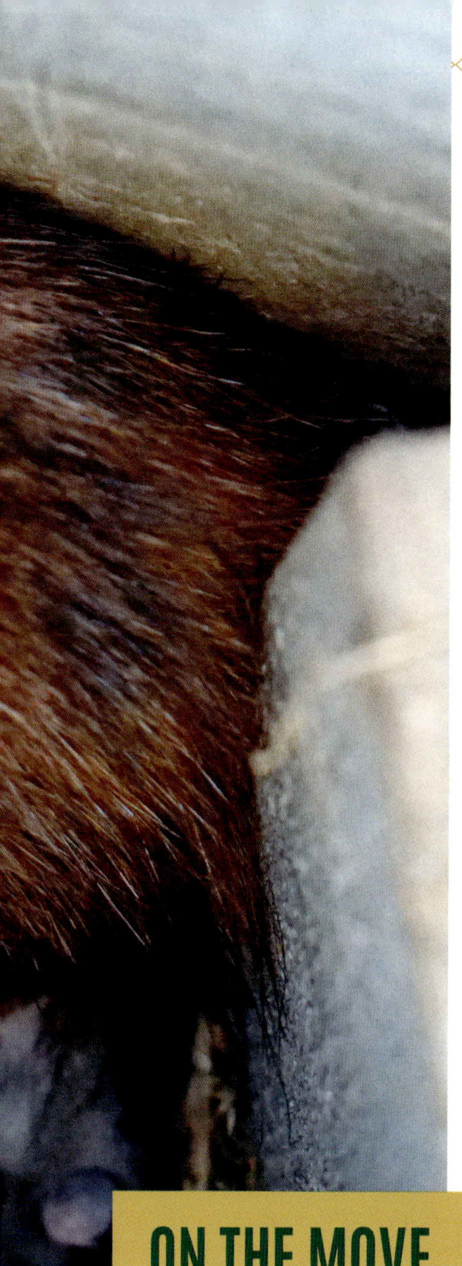

Mice and rats reproduce fast. So, an infestation can get out of control quickly. A female mouse can start giving birth when she is just two months old. And she can have 10 babies every few weeks. Rats can give birth at a young age, too. They can have as many as seven litters a year. And each litter can have a dozen babies.

ON THE MOVE

Mice and rats are native to Asia. But they spread as people traveled. For example, some stowed away on ships. Today, mice and rats live on nearly every continent. Antarctica is the only one without them.

Capybaras can weigh more than 140 pounds (64 kg).

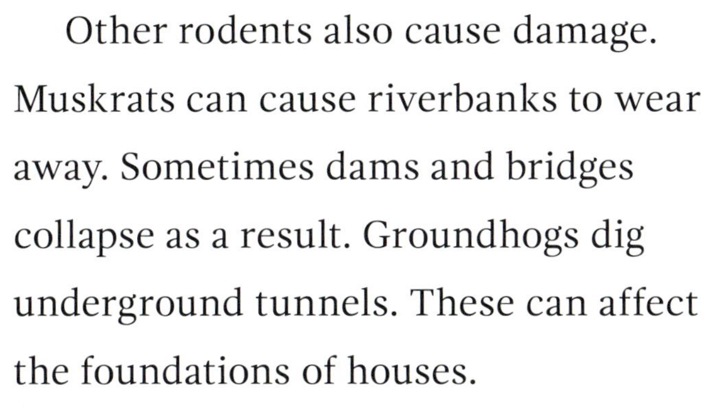

Other rodents also cause damage. Muskrats can cause riverbanks to wear away. Sometimes dams and bridges collapse as a result. Groundhogs dig underground tunnels. These can affect the foundations of houses.

GIANT RODENTS

In parts of South America, capybaras are pests. Capybaras are the world's largest rodents. They are the size of sheep. People moved into their habitats. Capybaras now raid some people's crops and gardens.

Chapter 3

RODENTS IN THE HOUSE

Rodents cause billions of dollars of damage every year. Mice and rats cause the most damage to buildings. These rodents are most likely to enter people's spaces.

In the United States, rodents sneak into about 21 million homes every year.

Chipmunks often burrow under houses, patios, and decks. Their digging can lead to damage.

Mice and rats cause many problems in buildings. They pee and poop everywhere. A rat leaves up to 50 droppings every day. A mouse can double that. Droppings ruin clothes and other belongings.

NOT JUST RATS AND MICE

Other rodents can also cause trouble in homes. Squirrels and chipmunks are two examples. They may build nests in attics or crawl spaces. That can damage insulation.

Mice and rats also cause damage by gnawing. All rodents have two pairs of large front teeth. These teeth are called incisors. They are sharp and hard. And they never stop growing. Rodents keep these teeth short by chewing. Their chewing can be very destructive.

MONEY TROUBLE

In 2018, a rat crawled into a cash machine in India. The rat jammed the machine. It chewed up nearly $18,000 worth of money.

Nutria are pests in many US states. They are known for their yellow or orange front teeth.

Mice and rats can enter homes in many ways. They may chew holes to get inside.

Mice and rats chew on nearly anything. They chew through wood, plastic, and even aluminum. They can damage pipes, walls, furniture, and floors. Some even chew electric wiring and gas lines. This damage costs a lot of money to fix. It also increases the risk of fires. That happened to an Ohio family in 2022. A blaze broke out in their house. The fire was caused by mice. They had chewed on electrical wires.

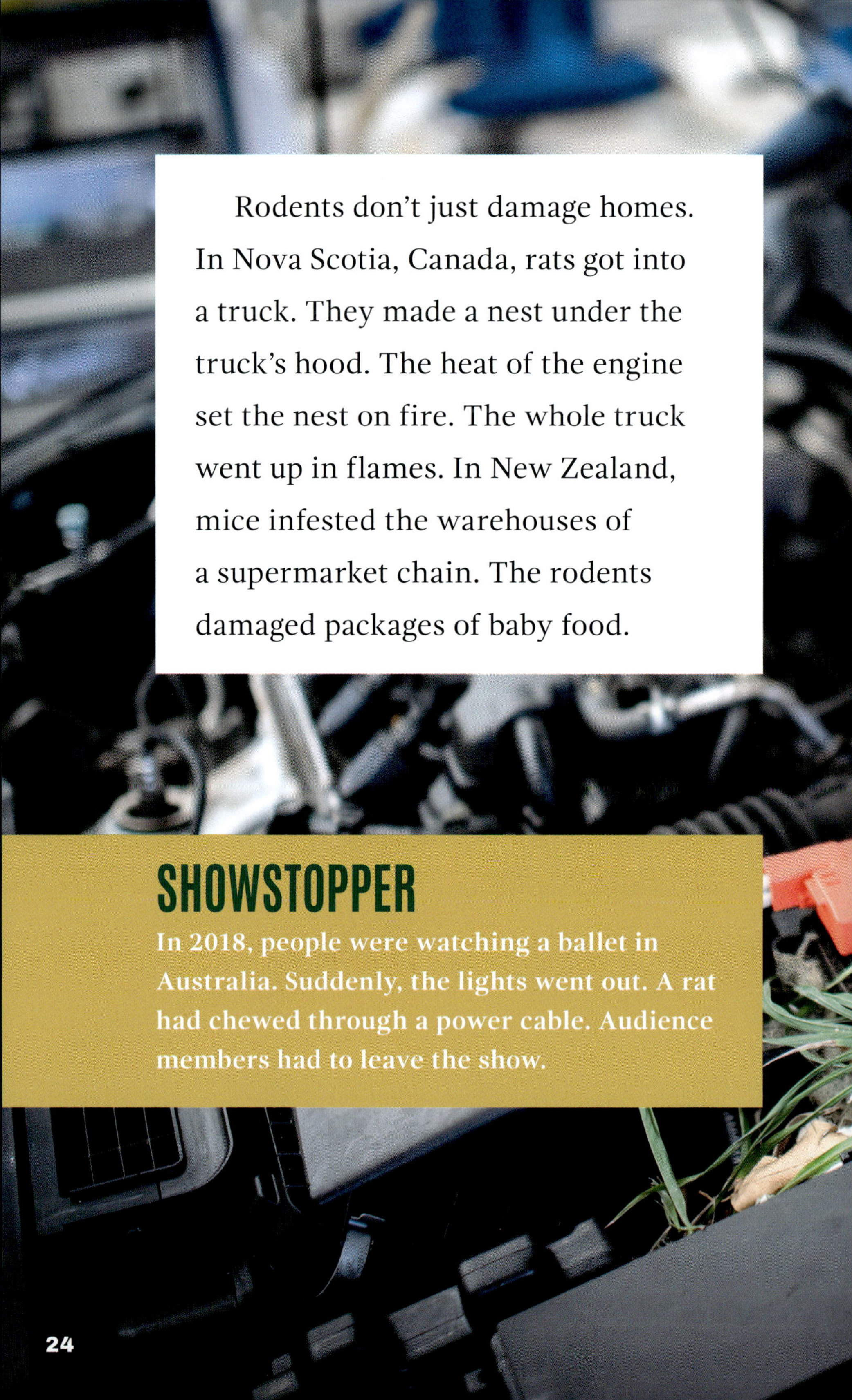

Rodents don’t just damage homes. In Nova Scotia, Canada, rats got into a truck. They made a nest under the truck’s hood. The heat of the engine set the nest on fire. The whole truck went up in flames. In New Zealand, mice infested the warehouses of a supermarket chain. The rodents damaged packages of baby food.

SHOWSTOPPER

In 2018, people were watching a ballet in Australia. Suddenly, the lights went out. A rat had chewed through a power cable. Audience members had to leave the show.

Mice can make nests all over. Some popular nesting places include dryers, ovens, and cars.

Every year, rodents destroy about 20 percent of the world's food supply.

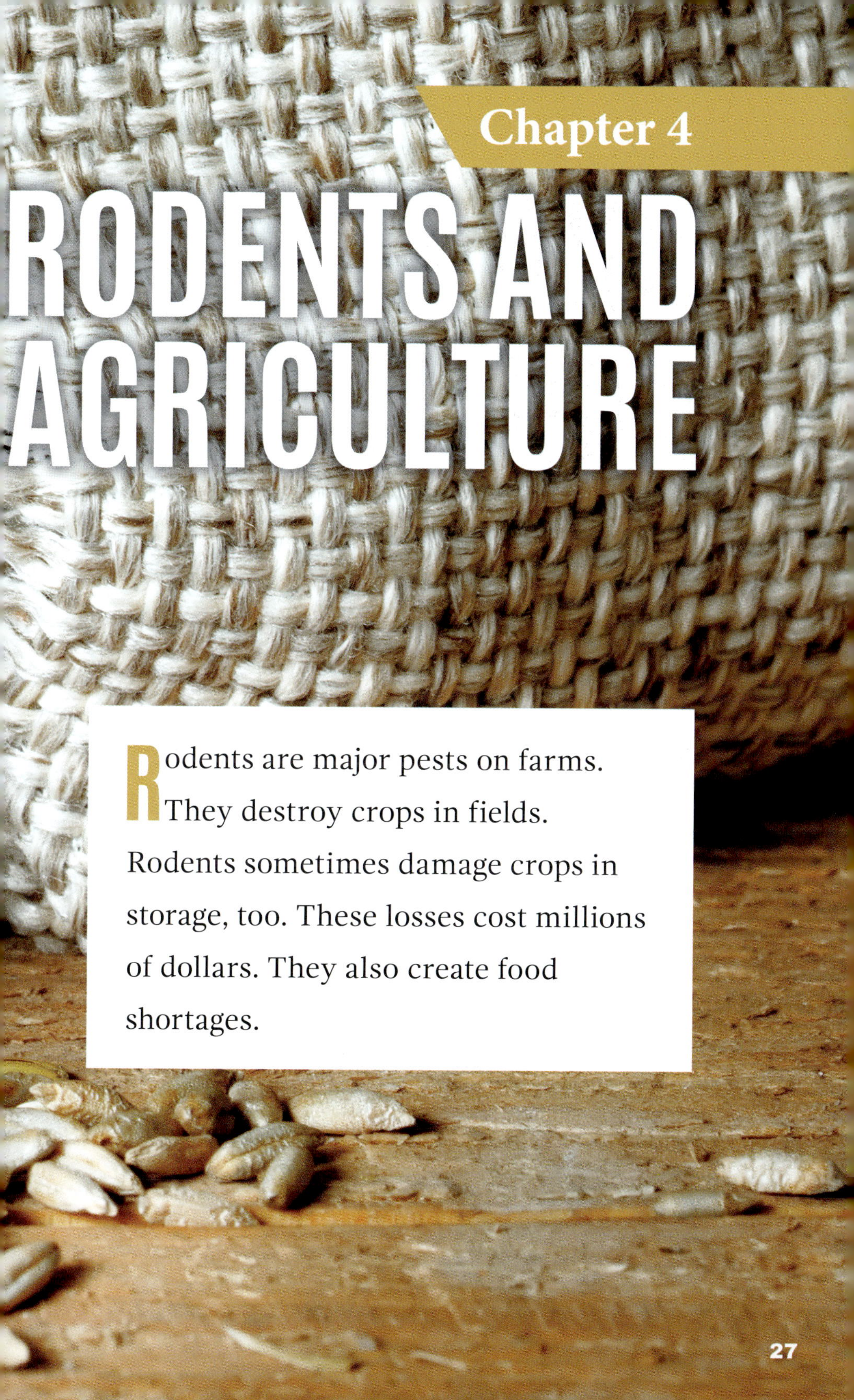

Chapter 4

RODENTS AND AGRICULTURE

Rodents are major pests on farms. They destroy crops in fields. Rodents sometimes damage crops in storage, too. These losses cost millions of dollars. They also create food shortages.

In Indonesia, rats are a big problem for rice farmers. Rats eat the rice growing in fields. They also poop and pee in stored rice. That ruins it. This happens in other parts of Asia, too. The amount of rice lost could feed more than 200 million people.

FEAST, THEN FAMINE

A certain type of bamboo grows in Mizoram, India. Every 50 years, it grows flowers. The flowers produce seeds, which rats like to eat. As a result, rat populations increase. Millions of rats eat the seeds. When the seeds are gone, rats eat farmers' crops. This causes a famine.

Some farmers lose half of their rice to rodents each year.

In Africa, there are about 400 kinds of rodents. But only a few species cause trouble for farmers. One is called the multimammate mouse. Many farmers in East Africa lose crops to these rodents. In Tanzania, outbreaks have destroyed entire harvests.

RODENTS VS. CHICKENS

Rodents don't just go after farmers' crops. Mice and rats also sneak into chicken houses. They eat the chicken feed. Even more feed gets ruined by their droppings. Rodents chew on equipment, too.

One rodent pest in Africa is the Nile rat. These rats destroy many grains in Tanzania.

When it rains, rodents try to find shelter. They may enter homes when there's lots of rain.

Scientists believe climate change is making rodent problems worse. Many rodents thrive in warmer weather. In addition, climate change can cause more rain. And when there's a lot of rain, rodents breed very quickly. That's because more plants grow. This means extra food for the rodents.

LAST RESORT

Chisumbanje, Zimbabwe, received more rain than usual in 2022. The rain helped lots more plants grow. That brought large numbers of rodents. Many farmers lost all their crops. People didn't have enough to eat. They had no choice but to hunt and eat the rodents.

Rodents are also a problem for farmers in wealthy countries. But they usually don't cause food shortages. These countries tend to have extra food stored away. Their governments also have more money. This money can help farmers. In 2021, rodents affected farmers in New South Wales, Australia. The area's government helped. It gave farmers poison bait and money.

A plane drops poison bait over an Australian field to control mice.

That's Wild!

MICE BY THE MILLIONS

In 2021, millions of mice swarmed farms in Australia. The outbreak lasted for six months. Farmers caught thousands of mice every day.

The rodents invaded haystacks. They raided grain silos. They chewed through cropland. Mice damaged farm vehicles, too. They even chewed up a phone company's equipment. Then some farming towns lost phone service.

The damage cost hundreds of millions of dollars. Similar events take place every few years in Australia. They are driven by weather patterns.

People got sick during the mouse outbreak in Australia. The mice also bit people.

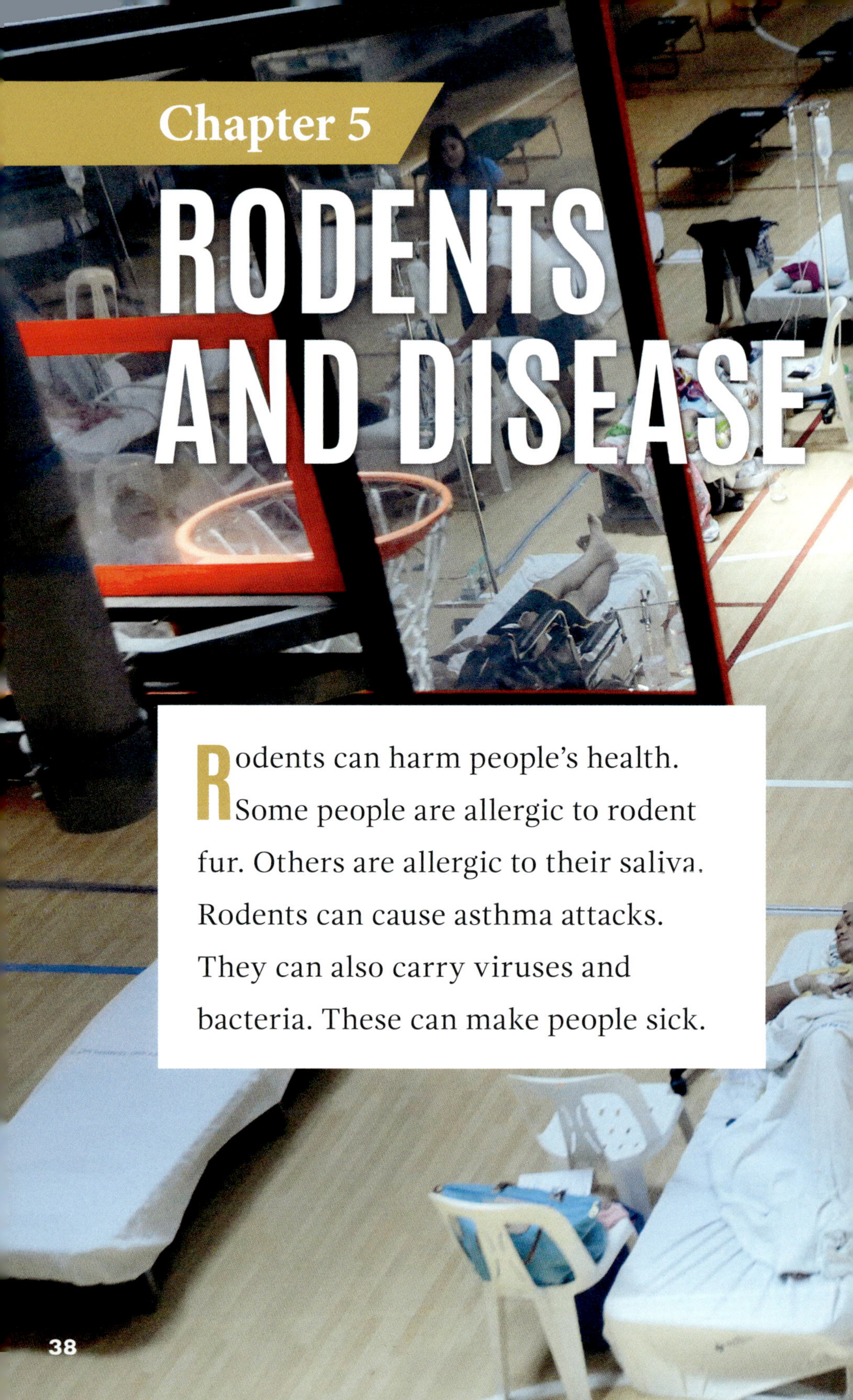

Chapter 5

RODENTS AND DISEASE

Rodents can harm people's health. Some people are allergic to rodent fur. Others are allergic to their saliva. Rodents can cause asthma attacks. They can also carry viruses and bacteria. These can make people sick.

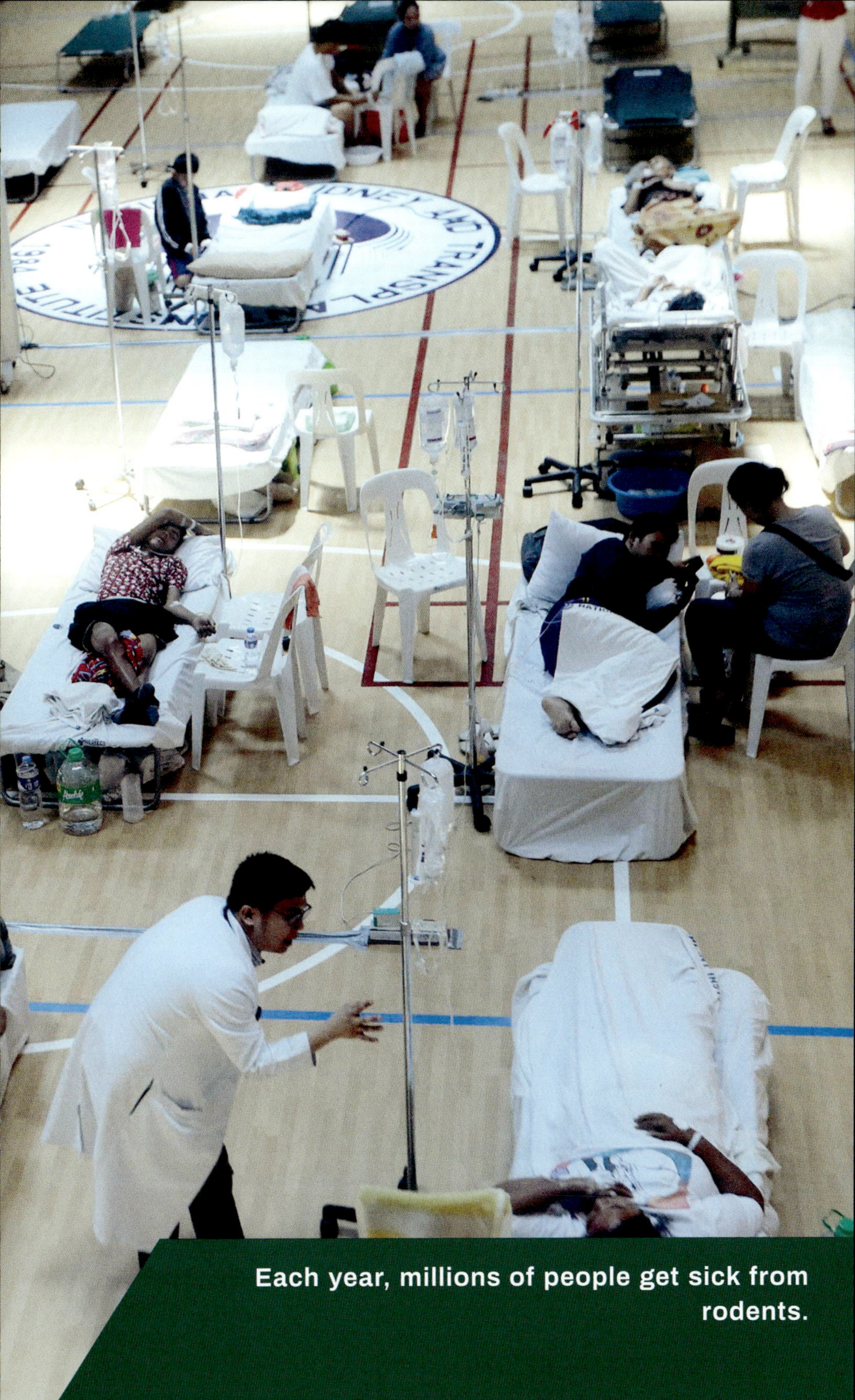

Each year, millions of people get sick from rodents.

Some diseases spread indirectly. For example, a rodent might be carrying a virus. Then an insect bites the rodent. The insect picks up the virus. Then it bites a person. It gives the person the rodent's virus.

More than 60 different diseases can spread to humans from rodents.

DEADLY RODENTS

In 2012, several people got sick at a national park in California. They got hantavirus. This disease is serious. It harms people's lungs. Three people died. Five others went to the hospital. The sickness was traced to rodents. They had been in the cabin where the people stayed.

Many white-footed mice carry Lyme disease.

Lyme disease spreads indirectly. This disease causes fever and aches. It can make people extremely tired. It can also affect the heart, joints, and nervous system. Bacteria causes Lyme disease. Mice sometimes carry this bacteria. Ticks bite the mice. They pick up the bacteria. Then ticks spread it to people.

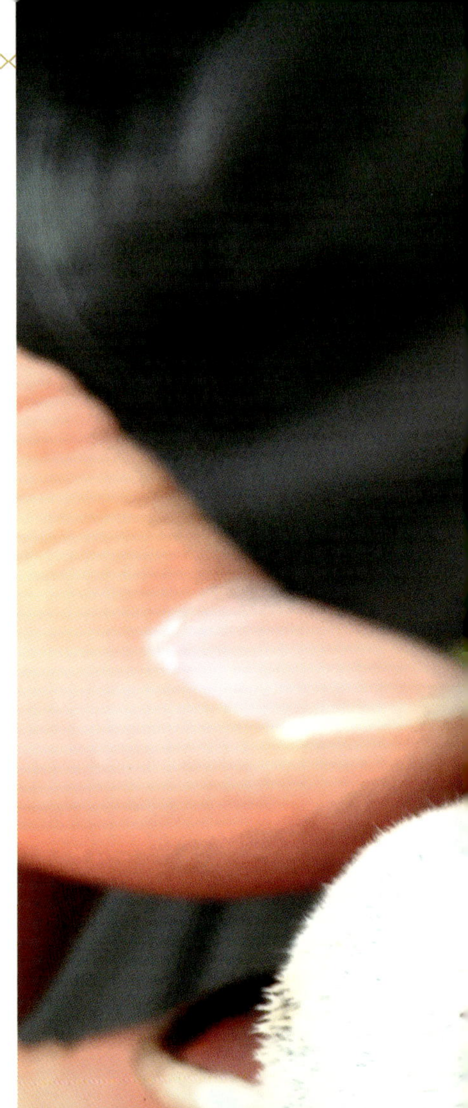

Rodents spread other diseases directly. Bites are one way. Most rodents try to stay away from people. But some rodents bite if they feel threatened. Others bite if they are very hungry. Bacteria or viruses may be in rodents' mouths. As a result, bites can spread diseases to people.

RATS ATTACK

In 2023, rats bit a sleeping baby in Indiana. The rats chewed off parts of the baby's fingers. They also bit his face more than 50 times. The baby lost a lot of blood. He received new blood at the hospital. The baby barely survived.

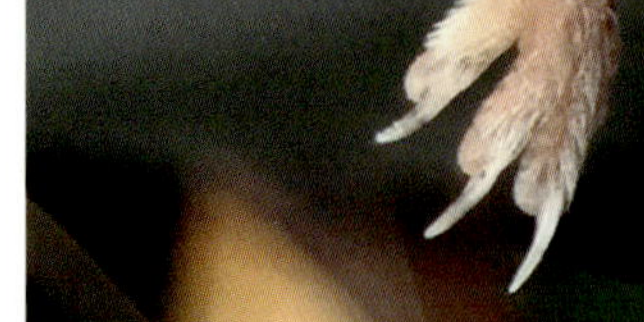

Up to 40,000 people get bitten by rats every year in the United States.

Rodents' waste can spread disease, too. It can contain bacteria and viruses. Rodents might poop or pee in food or water. People don't always know about it. So, they drink or eat it. Then they get sick. One disease is called leptospirosis. It harms people's kidneys and lungs. Rats can spread it through their urine.

LASSA FEVER

Rat droppings and urine can spread Lassa fever. This disease can cause massive bleeding. It can lead to deafness. Sometimes people die. In 2023, this disease spread in Nigeria. More than 200 people lost their lives.

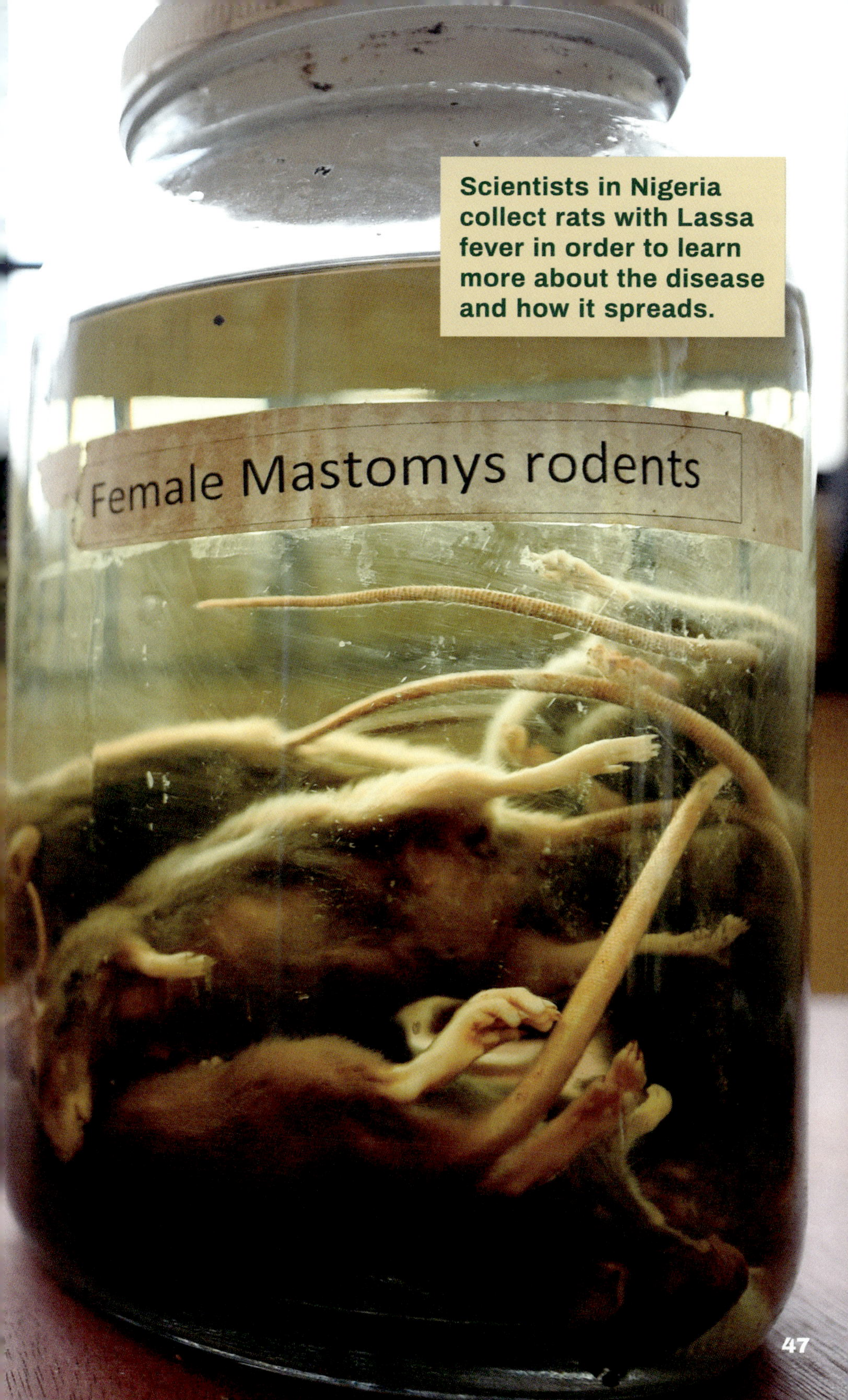

Scientists in Nigeria collect rats with Lassa fever in order to learn more about the disease and how it spreads.

That's Wild!

THE BUBONIC PLAGUE

The bubonic plague was a deadly disease. In the 1300s, it spread through Europe. People got fevers, chills, and threw up. Parts of their body swelled painfully.

In the 1700s, the plague spread across China. In 1894, it began going around the world. It killed more than 10 million people.

Rats helped spread the plague. They carried a type of bacteria. Fleas bit those rats. Then those fleas bit humans.

Some people still get the plague today. But modern medicine can treat the illness.

The bubonic plague was spread by black rats.

Chapter 6

MANAGING THE ISSUE

Rodents can be hard to control. Some people use traps and bait to catch them. Others use smart devices with sensors. These devices make noise. That scares away rodents when they get close.

People use cages to trap animals. After a rodent enters the cage, the door closes.

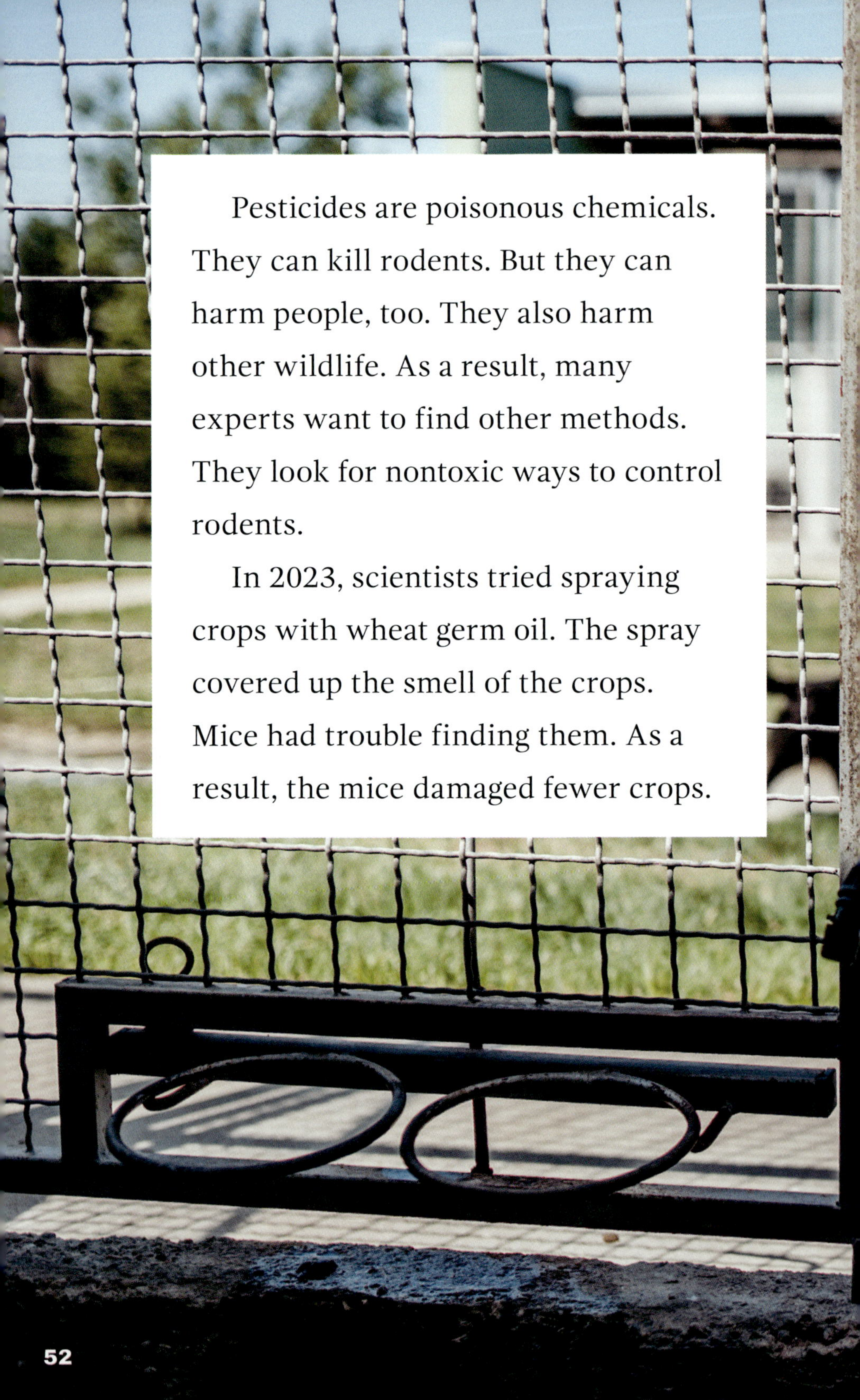

Pesticides are poisonous chemicals. They can kill rodents. But they can harm people, too. They also harm other wildlife. As a result, many experts want to find other methods. They look for nontoxic ways to control rodents.

In 2023, scientists tried spraying crops with wheat germ oil. The spray covered up the smell of the crops. Mice had trouble finding them. As a result, the mice damaged fewer crops.

Rat poison can harm the environment. It can also make pets sick.

Some cities kill rats with carbon monoxide. Workers find rat burrows. They pump the gas into them. After a while, the rats can't breathe. But the gas goes away over time. That makes it safer than poison bait or pesticides.

NO MORE RAT BABIES

In 2023, one city in Michigan gave rats birth control. Workers put the medicine in rat burrows. Rats ate it. Then they could not have babies. The medicine was nontoxic. So, it was not harmful.

Burrows are holes and tunnels that rats live in. A burrow typically has eight rats.

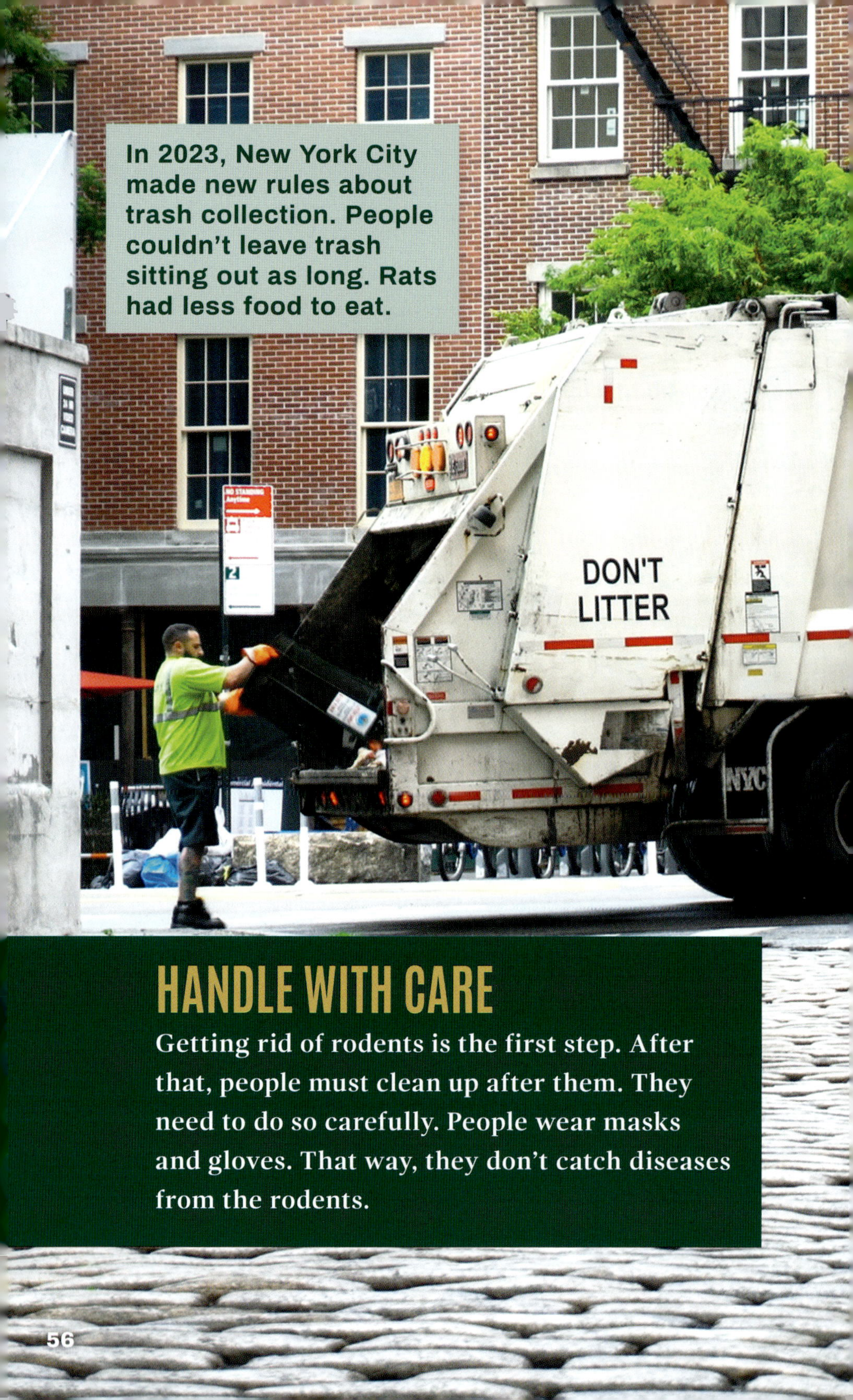

In 2023, New York City made new rules about trash collection. People couldn't leave trash sitting out as long. Rats had less food to eat.

HANDLE WITH CARE

Getting rid of rodents is the first step. After that, people must clean up after them. They need to do so carefully. People wear masks and gloves. That way, they don't catch diseases from the rodents.

Preventing rodents is the best method. People can fix cracks and holes in buildings. That helps keep rodents out. People can also clean up trash. That cuts down on rats' food sources.

MAP

1. Michigan, United States: City officials give rats birth control to limit their numbers.
2. New York, United States: To control rats, a mayor puts in place new rules to reduce trash in the streets.
3. Nova Scotia, Canada: A family's truck catches fire after mice nest in the engine.

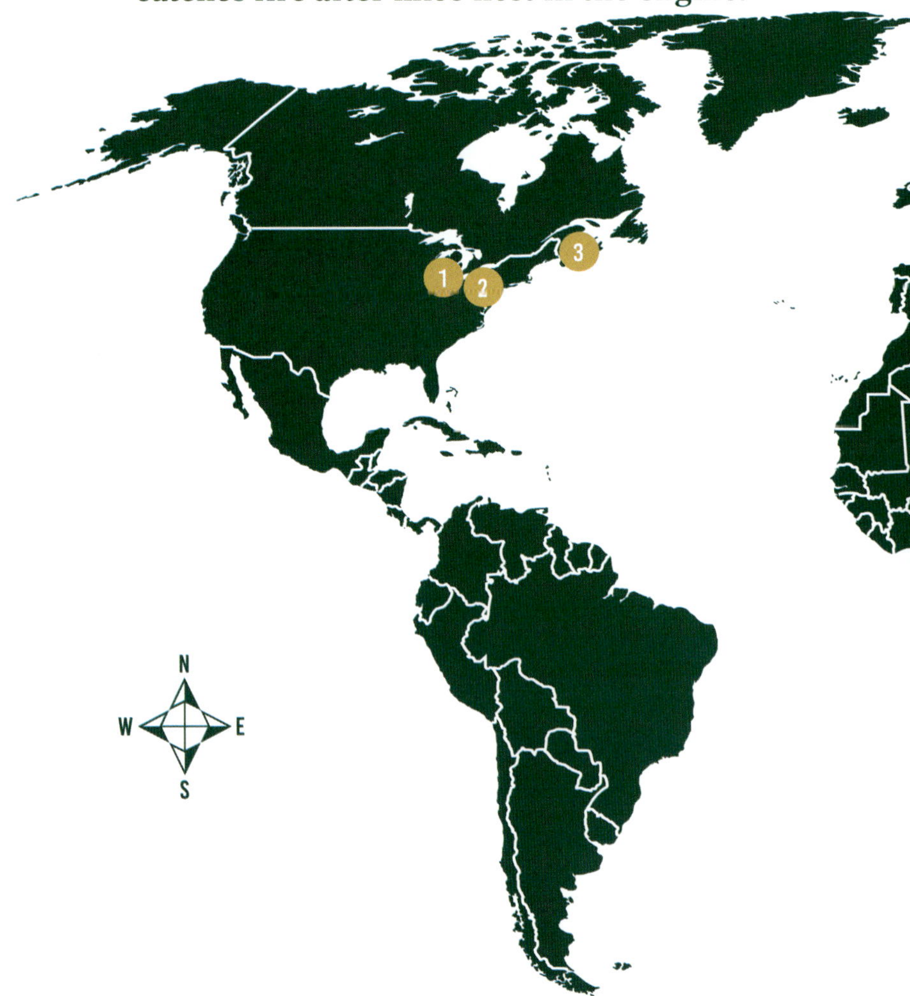

4 Manicaland, Zimbabwe: A huge rodent outbreak destroys farmers' crops. People are forced to eat the rodents instead.

5 Assam, India: A rat crawls into a cash machine and destroys nearly $18,000.

6 New South Wales, Australia: The government sets aside money for farmers affected by rodents.

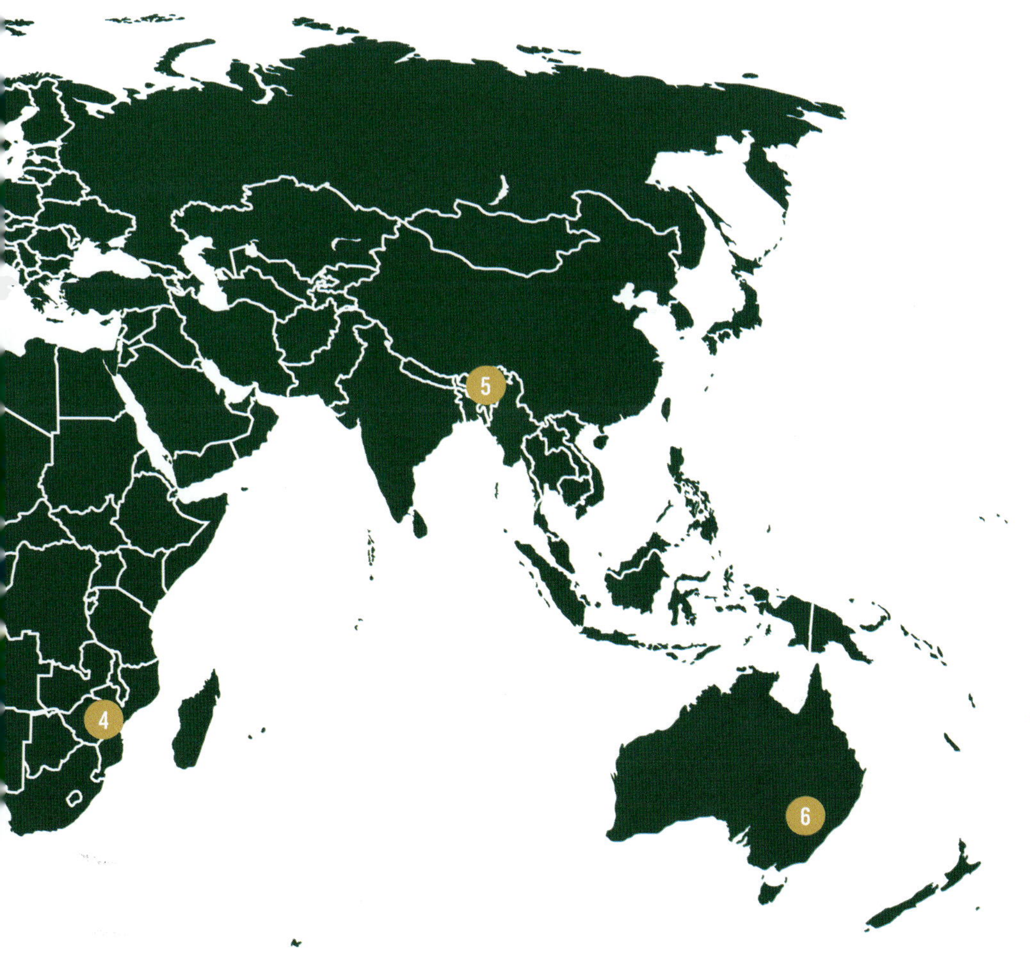

COMPREHENSION QUESTIONS

Write your answers on a separate piece of paper.

1. Write a paragraph explaining why rodent populations can get out of control so fast.

2. If you found rodent droppings in your home, what would you do?

3. Which disease killed up to half of the people in Europe in the 1300s?

   A. bubonic plague
   B. hantavirus
   C. Lyme disease

4. What kind of weather patterns might increase mouse outbreaks in Australia?

   A. weather that is drier than usual
   B. weather that is windier than usual
   C. weather that is rainier than usual

5. What does **gnawing** mean in the text?

*Mice and rats also cause damage by **gnawing**. All rodents have two pairs of large front teeth.*

A. chewing

B. soiling

C. infesting

6. What does **harvests** mean in the text?

*Many farmers in East Africa lose crops to these rodents. In Tanzania, outbreaks have destroyed entire **harvests**.*

A. times when farmers sell food

B. times when farmers plant seeds

C. times when farmers pick crops

Answer key on page 64.

GLOSSARY

asthma
A medical condition that can make breathing difficult.

burrows
Tunnels or holes that animals use as homes.

exterminator
A person who gets rid of pests in homes or buildings.

famine
An extreme lack of food over a long period of time.

infestation
When many pests are somewhere they shouldn't be.

insulation
Materials that help keep the temperature of buildings steady.

litters
Groups of baby animals that are born at the same time.

nervous system
The body's system of long, thin fibers called nerves. Nerves carry information between the brain and other parts of the body.

species
Groups of animals or plants that are similar and can breed with one another.

thrive
To do extremely well.

TO LEARN MORE

BOOKS

Backhouse, Frances. *Beavers: Radical Rodents and Ecosystem Engineers*. Victoria, BC: Orca Book Publishers, 2021.

Huddleston, Emma. *Rats*. Mendota Heights, MN: Focus Readers, 2022.

Lim, Angela. *Rat Behavior*. Minneapolis: Abdo Publishing, 2023.

ONLINE RESOURCES

Visit **www.apexeditions.com** to find links and resources related to this title.

ABOUT THE AUTHOR

Elisabeth Herschbach is an editor and writer from Maryland who has written more than a dozen books for K–12 students.

INDEX

ANSWER KEY:

1. Answers will vary; 2. Answers will vary; 3. A; 4. C; 5. A; 6. C